"Hi. I'm Crystal."

An Introduction to Crystals for Children.

By Abbey Acevedo

Illustrated By Paz Ulloa

Copyright © 2021 Abbey Acevedo

All Rights Reserved

This book contains material protected under the International and Federal Copyright Laws and Treaties. Any unauthorized reprint or use of this material is prohibited. No portion of this book may be reproduced in any form or by means, electronic or mechanical, including photocopying, recording, or by any information storage retrieval system without written permission from the author.

For permissions please email: acevedo.abbey@gmail.com

Illustrations by Paz Ulloa

ISBN: 9798593764171

Acknowledgments

To my nieces and nephews: Sariah, Gracie, Mia, Pudge, Francis, Hunter S., Dahlin, Truman, Olivia, Eleanor, Isla, Madelyn, Danny, Noah, Yesmina, Caleb, Jayce, Sawyer, Hunter C., Hazel, and Valentina.

You are the true gems.

You can have, be, and do anything your heart desires.

I know you will not stay young forever, but I hope you stay forever young at heart.

XO, *Fauntie Abbey

*Fun Auntie

"Hi, I'm Crystal"

Hello there friend, how do you do?

My name is Crystal and I'm here for you.

I can help you sleep and help you think.

I come in all colors, like purple and pink.

I can be raw or polished, square, or round.

Bought in stores, or found in the ground.

Take this journey with me by turning the pages,

To discover how to use me in different emotional stages.

Fluorite

I am green & purple and I make your mind light.

I help you to learn and my name is Fluorite.

If your brain is foggy and you want it to be clear,

You will definitely want to keep me near.

There are some words you can say when you work with me,

So that you will have some mental clarity.

"I am smart, I am clever, I am always learning more.

I am bright, I am clear-headed, and I am always sure."

Lapis Lazuli

I am blue with specks of gold, and it is your truth that I hold.

I help bring the words inside you out into the world to be free.

I'm about self-expression and my name is Lapis Lazuli.

If you have trouble communicating or saying what's in your heart,

You'll want to have me close to you because I help you with that part.

Close your eyes and say this with me, and make sure to repeat it times three.

"I speak openly and clearly and I trust myself dearly.

I speak openly and clearly and I trust myself dearly.

I speak openly and clearly and I trust myself dearly."

Carnelian

I am reddish-brown and orange too, I kind of look like fires do.

I help you focus on the moment you're in, and my name is Carnelian.

If you need an energy boost or have forgotten who you are,

Hold me in your hands and I will remind you that you're a star.

I help improve your luck, and get your creative juices flowing,

So say these things below to keep your confidence growing.

"I am present and this day I will seize,

I share my gifts and talents with ease."

Amethyst

I am purple and clear, and the next time you want to make a fist,

I'll help you to release your anger and my name is Amethyst.

I have a calming effect, and can help ease your worries and your fears,

I can be tucked under your pillow to chase away nightmares.

I help you hear your inner voice, the one that's in your head,

And how to trust yourself so you know when to follow your heart instead.

I connect you to your very best self, so repeat after me if you want my help.

"I am whole, mind, body, and soul. I am safe and secure. I am balanced. I am at peace and I don't need anything more."

Rose Quartz

I am different shades of pink. I will be there for you when your heart hurts.

Because I love you unconditionally, and my name is Rose Quartz.

I help you to find peace and comfort and to release your stress.

I open up your heart so that you can feel the wonder of being blessed.

My love is so strong, it's a tidal wave of emotion,

And when I am with you, it will be like you're bathing in it as if you were in the ocean.

I help remind you that you are worthy and deserving,

And when we are together, it is humanity we are serving.

I don't need you to speak words out loud the way you did above.

I just need you to take deep breaths and remember that you are love.

"Hi, I'm Crystal"

Well, my friend, it's been so fun, I have had a blast!
If this was the first time you've heard of me, I hope it won't be the last.
There are many colors and shades and different sides to me,
Similar to the emotions you might be experiencing internally.

The next time you're feeling a certain way,
hold me in your hand and say what I taught you to say.
You will feel better, no doubt about it,
Your voice is a gift, so better yet, SHOUT IT!
I'll always be here for you, even if we don't talk.
I might be your crystal, but you will always be my rock.

THE END

(which is also a new beginning!)

Color with Crystal

How Are You Feeling Today?

Color with Crystal

How Are You Feeling Today?

Color with Crystal

How Are You Feeling Today?

Color with Crystal

How Are You Feeling Today?

Color with Crystal

How Are You Feeling Today?

Color with Crystal

How Are You Feeling Today?

Printed in Great Britain
by Amazon

CONTENTS

What is biomass?	6
Why do we need biomass?	8
What is agricultural residue?	10
Energy from animal waste	12
What is biogas?	14
Fuels from forests	16
Fuels from crops	18
What are biofuels?	20
Fuel from landfills	22
Problems with biomass	24
Current uses and future	26
Bioenergy in India	28
Glossary/Index	30

What is biomass?

What do we have in common with a tree and cow dung? We are all biomass! The word 'biomass' has two parts: 'bio', which means anything that is or has been alive, and 'mass', which is the total matter contained in a body.

▲ Algae is also a form of biomass.

That's all biomass

Biomass includes wood, leaves, flowers, seeds, tree bark, and even algae. Dead animals are also biomass. So are products from living animals, like cow dung. These products are called organic matter. They are renewable, which means that they will not get over and will continue to be replenished in nature. These can be used as fuel for energy. Things like plastic, metal, and glass are not biomass.

All biomass can be changed into solid, liquid or gaseous fuel. This fuel is called biofuel or agrofuel.

Down the ages

The way humans lived changed once they learned to use fire. This happened more than 1,500,000 years ago. The first fires burned twigs, branches, and dry leaves. Later, in went animal fat. Even today, dry animal dung is burnt to produce heat. In Tibet, the highest plateau in the world, yak dung is used for this purpose. In the Andes, llama excrement is a valuable product, and exchanged for other items. The pioneers who settled in North America in the early nineteenth century, used buffalo chips, or dung patties, since firewood was difficult to find.

Dry animal dung, like that of the cow, yak, llama, and other animals is burnt to generate heat.

Dust to dust, carbon to carbon

Plants take in energy from the sun, water from the soil, and carbon dioxide from the air to make food through photosynthesis. This is how carbon dioxide is fixed in plants and is transferred to animals that eat them. When animals eat plants, the energy from plants is passed on to them. The carbon is sent back into the atmosphere when we let out carbon dioxide with our breath and also when living things die and decay. This is called the carbon cycle because it goes round and round like the wheels of your bicycle.

Energy from the Lap of Nature

Sunlight
CO_2 in the air
Photosynthesis in plants
Animal respiration
Plant respiration
Primary consumers
Dead organisms and waste products

▲ The process by which carbon dioxide is fixed in plants, transferred to animals, and released back into the atmosphere is called the carbon cycle.

How dung gets done

Dung is leftover food digested by friendly bacteria. Wet dung is mixed with straw and other biomass. Then, it is made into little croquettes or patted on a wall. In a few days, the cakes dry into fuel called cow dung cakes or buffalo chips. Cow dung includes the waste from cows, ox, bullock, and buffalo.

Dung frisbee
In the 1800s in America, children played with frisbee-like devices, made from buffalo dung.

In many parts of the developing world, cow dung is used as a fertilizer and fuel.

Why do we need biomass?

What would you use to light a campfire? Twigs, dry branches, and leaves. All these are biomass. That's what people have been burning for light and heat for thousands of years. Today, biomass is being used for producing electricity.

Too hot to handle

Had it not been for greenhouse gases, we would have frozen. Life on the earth would not have been possible! Over the years, machines have got better and faster and have taken over almost all the work people and animals did. These machines need energy to work. Most of this energy comes from fossil fuels. So, the use of fossil fuels has gone up. This is making the earth much too warm. This is harmful for the planet and its inhabitants in many ways.

The increased use of fossil fuels over the years has led to excessive heating of the earth.

Fossil fuels

Coal and petroleum are formed over millions of years from the remains of plants, animals, and other organisms, which lived in another era. These remains were buried deep under great pressure, or fossilized. That is why they are called fossil fuels.

People began to use coal to melt metals about four thousand years go. Petroleum, or crude oil, was discovered around the same time. However, when fossil fuels are burnt, they let off greenhouse gases like carbon dioxide, methane, and nitrous oxide, which trap the heat of the sun in the earth's atmosphere and make it warm.

Prehistoric humans used twigs and branches to light fire.

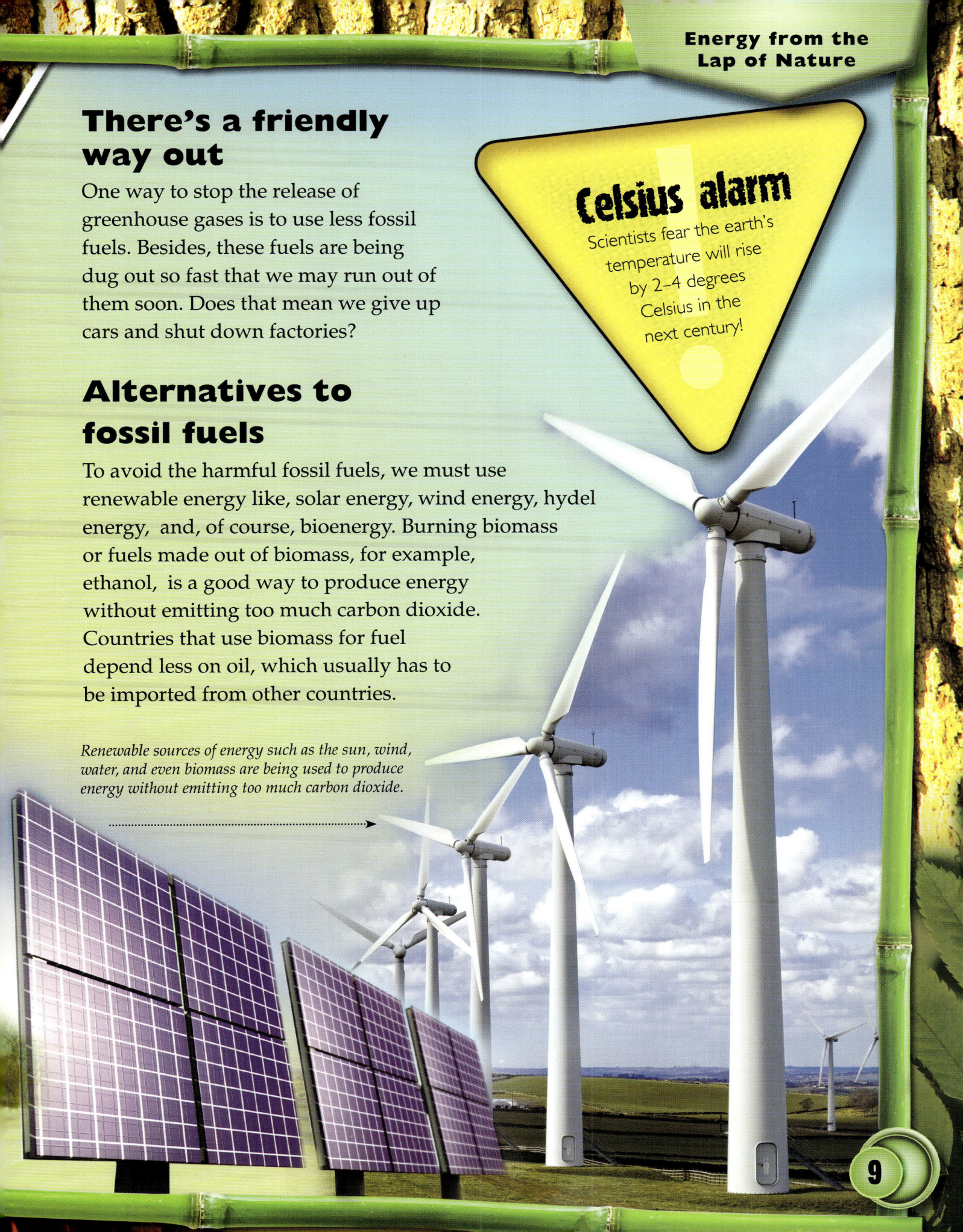

Energy from the Lap of Nature

There's a friendly way out

One way to stop the release of greenhouse gases is to use less fossil fuels. Besides, these fuels are being dug out so fast that we may run out of them soon. Does that mean we give up cars and shut down factories?

Alternatives to fossil fuels

To avoid the harmful fossil fuels, we must use renewable energy like, solar energy, wind energy, hydel energy, and, of course, bioenergy. Burning biomass or fuels made out of biomass, for example, ethanol, is a good way to produce energy without emitting too much carbon dioxide. Countries that use biomass for fuel depend less on oil, which usually has to be imported from other countries.

Celsius alarm

Scientists fear the earth's temperature will rise by 2–4 degrees Celsius in the next century!

Renewable sources of energy such as the sun, wind, water, and even biomass are being used to produce energy without emitting too much carbon dioxide.

What is agricultural residue?

Remember that falling leaf you tried to catch to make a wish? Dry leaves are precious for other reasons too. Every part of a plant can produce energy. Energy can be produced from different types of agricultural or plant-based biomass. These include wood residue, sugar cane bagasse, energy crops, grass, and even waste paper. These are known as agricultural residues.

Energy crops and residues

Energy crops are grown for fuel. These include food crops like corn and sugar cane. Energy crops can also be non-food plants like poplar trees and switchgrass. These are agricultural, or crop, residues. Wood residues include twigs and branches, bits of wood left over after trees are cut for timber, and even chips left over at sawmills and paper mills. Bagasse gets its name from the Spanish word *'bagazo'*, meaning pulp. Bagasse is the crushed fibre of the sugar cane plant after the juice has been pressed out of it.

Biofuels are being produced from various crops, as well as non-food plants.

Use it all!

Remains of crops are made into pellets or chips, larger pieces are kept in stacks or bales. Straw is an agricultural residue. It is the dry part of what is left after grains are removed from a cereal plant. The stalks of plants that give us rice, wheat, corn, flax, and rye are made into straw. Most of this straw is burnt as fuel. It can also be used to make ethanol, a liquid fuel. The next time you bite into a cob of corn, remind yourself how useful the whole plant is—the stalks and straw, called stover, are made into biofuels. Wheat straw, rice straw, and nut hulls are also sources of biofuels.

Energy from the Lap of Nature

Biogas digesters that use both cow dung and water hyacinth produce about 22 per cent more biogas than those that use only dung.

Burning alcohol

While agricultural residue can be used as fuel in much the same way like you would burn it in a bonfire, it is more useful when it is fermented and turned into ethanol, an alcohol. Fermentation turns sugar in agricultural residue into alcohol, which can be used as fuel.

Chestnut, which grows in the temperate regions of the Northern Hemisphere, is also used for extracting biofuel.

Energy from weeds

Even plants like water hyacinth, which is frowned upon as a weed, are harvested for biomass. At a production plant in Kochi, India, a seven-hundred-litre tank holds water hyacinth pulp. It gives 3,600 litres of biogas, which is used to cook food. Nothing is wasted. Even the leftover mush is used as a fertilizer!

Energy from animal waste?

All kinds of biomass have been used to produce bioenergy. Every being, alive or dead, stores energy from the sun. We know now that any plant, from towering trees to algae and even pesky weeds like water hyacinth, can give us bioenergy. All kinds of animal waste, too, can give us bioenergy.

Dung has been used over the ages as fuel.

The wealth in waste

The dung of cows, pigs, and buffaloes is used to produce heat and electricity.

For thousands of years, waste has got a raw deal from humankind. Although dung has been used as fuel and given fancy names like landmine, meadow muffin, and surprise a la cow, we have treated leftovers from our farms and backyards as unwanted muck. Once we understood the carbon cycle, we knew that energy that we use to grow and do work is stored inside us. Now we know that nothing really is waste. It could just be that we haven't recognized the wealth within!

Energy from the Lap of Nature

What's hot, what's not?

All waste is wealth. Most animal wastes, or droppings, give out a lot of methane. This is a greenhouse gas. So, if the waste is left to rot, the methane goes up into the atmosphere, where it traps more heat and makes the planet warmer. Wouldn't it be wonderful if we could use this methane, which is a flammable, or fire-friendly, gas? It is actually being used! The droppings of chickens, as well as dung of pigs, cows, and buffaloes, can be used to produce gas, which can, in turn, be used for heating and generating electricity.

Wanted: dead or alive

Even animal offal, or the internal organs of animals farmed for food, can be used as fuel. For hundreds of years, people have wondered what to do with the offal. It was fed to other animals like dogs or simply thrown away. But this bio-waste is an important source of energy. And this use saves a lot of money spent in disposing of waste from slaughterhouses and poultries!

Bio-fact

Tallow, the hard fatty parts from animals, can be used with agricultural biomass like corn and soya bean to produce bio-diesel. In the United States, vehicles of the postal department and the military run on this kind of bio-diesel.

The camel is not only the ship of the desert, camel dung can be used as fuel in the treeless expanse.

What is biogas?

Biogas is a biofuel, or a gaseous fuel that is obtained from something that is or was once living. It can be produced from cattle dung manure, sewage, and the rubbish we throw out of our homes, or municipal solid waste, including leftover food, and also from specially grown energy crops like jatropha. Biogas is about 55–65 per cent methane and 45–35 per cent carbon dioxide. This gas can be used for cooking, lighting, and producing electricity.

Cheap and clean

Setting up and running a biogas plant is not very expensive. The fuel is clean, and it can heat and light our homes and streets and even be used for cooking. It can be treated, compressed, and used to drive cars! Biogas is a clever way to use garbage. It is also the answer to the shortage of space for garbage landfills, which give out dangerous methane gas. So far, four million biogas plants have been installed in India. Industries located in the Ankleshwar industrial area in the north-western state of Gujarat use the biogas produced from their own units.

Biogas plants can be set up anywhere. The fuel produced in the plant is clean and can be used for cooking.

Energy from the Lap of Nature

Chomp, chomp!

Waste from animals mixed with water is put into a digester, through an inlet pipe of the biogas plant. The digester sounds like a magic hat, but it is really an airtight container. The manure and waste water are fed into the digester pit, where some bacteria get busy, breaking down the matter and releasing biogas. An outlet pipe leads the gas out from the digester to wherever it needs to be used. Biogas is almost smoke free, and since it has no smell, you'd never suspect what it was before the microbes got working on it!

Here's to poop power!

In 2006, Japanese scientists made gasoline from cattle dung under high heat and pressure. With about 551,155 tonnes of cattle dung a year to use, that's a lot of fuel for Japan! In Texas, America, biomass like cotton gin from factories is combined with cow dung to produce fuel. Sulabh International, India, is the largest organization in the world working on sanitation. It uses human excreta to make biogas. The waste passes from the toilet to an underground anaerobic digester, which has an outlet chamber.

Waste not!
More than two million homes in India use cattle dung for biogas. In Sweden, a train runs on compressed biogas! In 2003, biogas lit about 19,000 houses in New Zealand.

Sorghum, a plant from semi-arid regions, is also being used to produce biogas.

Fuels from forests

Forests are carbon sinks. Trees give out oxygen and soak in huge amounts of carbon dioxide when they make food through photosynthesis. For millions of years, forests have given us fuel too. Red Riding Hood may have been gobbled up by the big bad wolf had not the woodcutter, who saved her, been looking for firewood! Sadly, people forget how long trees take to grow. They also forget how important forests are for the planet. In the past hundred years or so, more forests have been chopped down than ever before.

The willow is a fast-growing tree.

Cultivation forests

Ideally, trees should not be cut. But we need trees for timber. One solution is eco-forestry, or caring for a forest and trying to control how much of a forest is cleared at one time. Some countries grow fast forests or plantations. In these forests, or short rotation coppices, fast-growing trees like willow, maple, black walnut, green ash, sycamore, and poplar are cultivated in about three to five years. New trees grow from the stubs.

If you live in Austin, United States, you probably use electricity made from wood residue by the Green Mountain Energy Company.

Energy from the Lap of Nature

Don't let it go waste

When trees are cut for furniture, plywood, paper, and construction, much of the wood remains unused. In Australia, about half the timber is wasted. In Sweden, about 45 per cent timber is left behind. If left to decay, it will release methane, a greenhouse gas. This remnant wood and leafy tree tops can be used to produce biofuel.

The sycamore tree grows rapidly and can reach a height of sixty to hundred feet in a very short duration.

Wood ash can also be used as fertilizer.

Making the most of it

Sweeping up the forest floor reduces the risk of a forest fire. So, sawdust, bark, tree tops, and thin branches that are left behind by lumberjacks are converted into biofuels like wood gas, methanol or ethanol. Wood residues can be burnt to heat the air, and the steam generated can be used to dry timber or to produce electricity. Pulp mills use black liquor, or what is left behind from making paper, to heat the plant and for generating electricity.

Chip off the old block

Slough Heat and Power Station, United Kingdom, generated electricity from coal for about 80 years. Now, it uses wood chips to generate electricity, which is used in parks, plant nurseries, and schools.

Fuels from crops

For thousands of years, people have taken grains from crops and used the stalks as fuel. With the demand for power and fuel shooting up, scientists are growing energy crops, which are especially used for producing fuel.

Make hay while the sun shines!

Leafy energy crops are harvested when they are about three years old. These include elephant grass, bamboo, sweet sorghum, wheatgrass, and common switchgrass of the American Prairies, which are used for making hay; oilseeds like soya bean, sunflower, and canola; sugar crops like sugar beet, sugar cane, and sweet sorghum; starch crops like corn, soya bean, and maize; and oil-producing plants like jatropha and algae. All of these give us biofuels like ethanol and bio-diesel, which can be used in almost any diesel engine. B20, a blend of 20 per cent biofuel and 80 per cent diesel, is used in diesel engines.

Hide it under a bushel, oh no!

A bushel (about 35.2 litres) of soya bean can produce 5.2 litres of bio-diesel.

Some crops such as wheatgrass, switchgrass, and hay also give us biofuels such as ethanol and bio-diesel.

Energy from the Lap of Nature

Oil's well that ends well

The advantage of bio-diesel is that it can be produced from the crop most easily available in a country. In the United States, it is soya bean. In Brazil, it is castor oil. In Malaysia, coconut oil, and in Thailand, palm oil. In Greece, cotton seed is used, while in Spain, it is linseed. Even vegetable oil that we use for cooking can be used as fuel. Engine makers like MAN Diesel, Deutz Ag, and Wartsila have engines that run on cooking oil! Used vegetable oil is made into bio-diesel. This means that any oil left over after frying your favourite fish and chips need not be thrown away. About 100,000 tonnes of extra bio-diesel is being made in United Kingdom every year.

Bio-diesel can be produced from a variety of oils, including castor and palm oil.

The green oil well

Jatropha has been called the oil well plant. It is not choosy and grows in different kinds of soils—in dry land and waterlogged places. Cattle don't seem to like it, so the plant has a great time growing undisturbed. It lives for almost fifty years! The oil-filled seeds pop up when the plant is a year old. The oil extracts can run a diesel engine. Another wonder tree is the Indian birch, or *karanj*.

The seeds of jatropha contain almost 40 per cent oil. They can be crushed, processed, and used in a standard diesel engine.

What are biofuels?

You could just put a lit match to biomass (and use it directly as fuel by burning it), or you could convert it into methanol, ethanol or bio-diesel. Bio-diesel is made from alcohols like ethanol and methanol, combined with vegetable or animal oil or other biomass. These biofuels can also be used for heating and generating electricity.

If you thought biofuels might slow you down, think again. Even Formula One cars run on 5.75 per cent biofuel.

Going vroom on methanol

Call it wood alcohol, carbinol or wood naphtha, methanol is the simplest alcohol and catches fire easily. It is used to make bio-diesel. Even the ancient Egyptians knew about methanol! Methanol is used as fuel in automobiles in sprint, drag racing, and racing cars like Champcars and in model aircraft. It is also used in anti-freeze.

Energy from the Lap of Nature

The sweet fuel

Ethanol, or ethyl alcohol, can be made from sugar crops like sugar cane and from starch crops like corn. These crops are fermented with yeast to produce ethanol, which can be added to almost any engine. Flexible fuel vehicles can use E85, which has 85 per cent ethanol and 15 per cent petroleum, or gasoline. Ethanol is a far cleaner fuel than petroleum. Using 10 per cent ethanol fuel, or E10, produces 26 per cent less greenhouse gases than using gasoline.

Syngas power

Solid biomass can be heated to give out a flammable, or fire-friendly, gas called syngas, or pyrolysis oil. The process, pyrolysis, is carried out without oxygen. This is better than burning the biomass, since this gas can be cleaned to remove any impurities. The clean gas can get a turbine spinning to produce electricity. However, it takes a lot of energy, and so, is still an expensive process.

Let's fire together

Woody biomass can be combined in a regular boiler with 85 per cent or less of coal and burned in a process called co-firing to generate energy. This reduces the use of fossil fuels. Co-firing not only uses up waste biomass but decreases harmful gases like carbon dioxide, along with nitrogen oxide and sulphur oxide, which cause smog and acid rain. The steam that is produced moves a turbine, which drives an electrical generator, which, in turn, produces electricity.

Brazil switches to ethanol
Most vehicles in Brazil run on E85 made from sugar. Soon, Brazil may stop importing petroleum.

Biomass can be used to generate electricity. This can reduce our dependence on fossil fuels.

Fuel from landfills

Waste from rapidly growing cities is usually dumped in landfills. These are large pits, usually on the outskirts of the city. Landfills may be storehouses of trash, but we are now recognizing them as gold mines of energy.

Landfills then and now

Early landfills were just dumps. Dirty water trickled down and polluted the groundwater and streams nearby. The ground also got poisoned. Modern landfills are lined with waterproof material. Compactors, similar to road rollers, crush the waste to save space. The waste is often covered with soil to keep rats, flies, and other insects away.

The whiff of trash

Landfills emit a smelly, flammable gas, which is different from natural gas and methane. It has about 40–60 per cent methane. Most of the rest is carbon dioxide. Small amounts of nitrogen, oxygen, water vapour, and other chemicals are also present in it. It is released when bacteria digest organic garbage.

A school that cares

The Ecology Club at Pattonville High School in Maryland Heights, Missouri, uses landfill gas to heat the school, saving about forty thousand dollars a year.

Landfills are the largest source of methane pollution caused by human activity.

Energy from the Lap of Nature

Trash to treasure

Landfill gas is cleaned by removing carbon dioxide and is fed into turbines to produce electricity. The clean gas is piped to industries as fuel or used in fuel cells. Methane from landfills can be converted into methyl alcohol, or methanol.

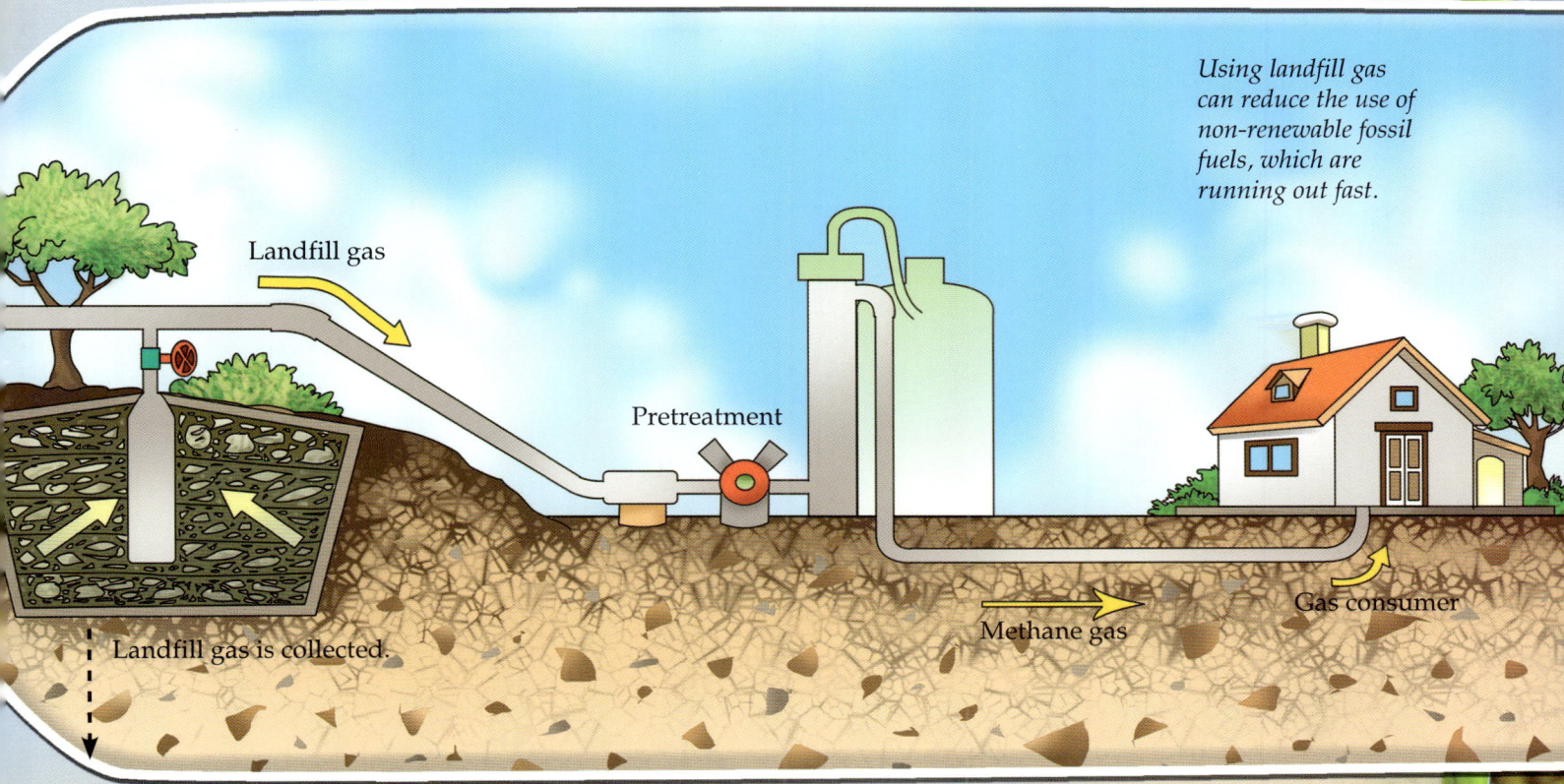

Using landfill gas can reduce the use of non-renewable fossil fuels, which are running out fast.

From fire to fuel

If allowed to escape, landfill gas increases air pollution. Its highly flammable nature makes it a dangerous gas if it is not handled carefully. In 1965, fire from landfill gas killed a boy in Los Angeles. On January 26, 1998, rubbish disposed of six metres below surface caught fire at Richard DeCoite's landfill in Ma'alaea, Hawaii, and smouldered for four months. Danbury, New Jersey, began to collect landfill gas in pipes after a fire in December 1996 raged on for weeks.

In 1994, the Landfill Methane Outreach Programme was started in the United States. Its efforts have resulted in a reduction in methane emissions equivalent to planting twenty-four million acres of forest or removing poisonous gases given out by seventeen million vehicles over a year. The best way to reduce landfill gas is to reduce garbage by reusing or recycling things.

Problems with biomass

Biomass may be the answer to fuel shortages and pollution. But nothing is perfect. There are problems of raw material prices, ethics of producing crops only for fuel, crop failure, pests, and increased pressure on land.

Costly crops

In December 2007, Natural Fuel Ltd of Australia stopped production at the country's largest bio-diesel plant because the price of palm oil had increased too much. Crops can be attacked and ruined. It also makes every litre of fuel more expensive. Sometimes, there simply isn't enough biomass to feed the fuel. factories.

Cough! splutter!

Biofuels like wood, crop leftovers, and dung are used as fuel by about half the world's population, generally the poor. Most of this biomass is burnt in open fires or in badly designed stoves. Often, biomass is lit inside the house, causing ten to hundred times more pollution than that from gas or electric stoves. These emissions include particulate matter, carbon monoxide, and nitrogen dioxide. People, especially women and small children who stay by the fire with their mother, suffer from breathing problems, burns, eye infections, and even cancer.

Biofuel costs can fluctuate, affecting fuel prices.

The poor in developing countries use biofuels like wood and dung for cooking food in traditional chulhas.

Energy from the Lap of Nature

Glug!

Genetically engineered crops could give us more biofuel, but they need more water. Now, that would add to our water woes!

Not all biofuels are absolutely clean. Some fuels like bio-diesel produce nitrogen oxide, which causes smog. A study conducted by Stanford University has shown that using an E85 blend of fuel emits ground-level ozone, which may increase respiratory diseases and ozone-related deaths.

Though genetically engineered crops can increase the yield of biofuels, they threaten native seeds, grasses, and trees and may lead to the extinction of entire species!

Diverting agricultural land for growing biofuel crops or using more and more of the produce for the manufacture of fuel will lead to food scarcity.

Where's my food?

Some biofuels are made from corn, soya bean, and canola, which are also used for food. The diversion of these crops to make biofuels may make food costlier. We will need more land to grow these crops. Rainforests are being destroyed in Malaysia and Indonesia for palm oil plantations and in Brazil, for sugar cane plantations. If biofuels were to become the only fuel we use, there would not be enough space to grow crops for our food after we grow energy crops for biofuels.

Dung fungus for biofuel

A fungus in elephant dung ferments wood sugars. Elephant dung is also used to make paper. If that dung is used to make biofuel, you'll have less poop paper to write on!

25

Current uses and future

Scientists and engineers are studying newer and better ways to make biofuels. They are trying to produce bio-diesel from algae, which is a storehouse of vegetable oil. As algae grow fast and do well in water, less land will be used up in cultivating them. Algae can produce about 15 times more oil per hectare than crops like palm, soya or jatropha.

More, improved biofuel, please!

Governments are putting in lots of money and effort to make more and better biofuels. Countries like Kazakhstan are already producing biofuels. The country's only biofuel plant can produce 57,000 tonnes of bio-ethanol every year. The International Energy Agency believes that 11 per cent of the energy the world uses comes from biomass. The United States is the largest producer of biopower, or electricity from biomass: 1.5 per cent of the total electricity supply, or forty-five billion kilowatt-hours of electricity. In Canada, biomass energy accounts for a greater share than energy from coal and nuclear power.

Creepy crawly oil

Scientists are also looking closely at termites that worm their way into wood and can chew up a tree. The process they use to turn wood into food could show us a way to turn wood into fuel. These tiny creatures are helped by bacteria in their stomach, which give out enzymes that dissolve the wood.

Termites, worms that feed on wood, provide a good example of turning wood into fuel.

Energy from the Lap of Nature

Smells like french fries

Tired of hearing that fast food isn't good for you? Well, all that extra oil can be put to good use. The only problem is that the smoke from the exhaust leaves you hungry: it smells of french fries! In 1997, Josh Tickell drove across America in a Winnebago run on used frying oil. The Veggie Van trundled more than forty thousand kilometres around the United States at 112 kilometres per hour and used about four litres of oil for every forty kilometres it travelled.

Trained to use biofuel

In December 2002, the Amritsar–Delhi Shatabdi train in India ran on diesel blended with 5 per cent bio-diesel. The Perambur Loco Works Laboratory, Chennai, uses 5 per cent bio-diesel in some trains and its shuttle passenger services. Its road vehicles run on a 20 per cent blend of biofuel and its passenger vehicle, on 100 per cent biofuel!

The Indian Railways is one of the largest rail networks in the world. It guzzles about forty million tonnes of diesel every year.

Wonder bacteria

Bacteria that are found in the stomach of termites can turn a sheet of paper into two litres of hydrogen.

Bioenergy in India

History of bioenergy in India

In India, biogas plants were developed for digesting cattle dung. However, over a period of time, new and improved technology was developed for various types of biomass materials. India has made progress in developing simple and easy-to-operate biogas plants. Some biogas plant models made in India are also being promoted in other countries. The first effort made in the field was in 1897. Biogas from human waste was utilized to meet lighting needs at the Matunga Leper Asylum in Bombay. In 1939, the technology to produce biogas from cattle dung was developed at the Indian Agricultural Research Institute, New Delhi.

Biogas plants provide clean fuel, which can be used for cooking as well as generating electricity.

Progress so far

In 1981–1982, a government-sponsored scheme was launched to promote the use of biogas in India. Known as the National Biogas and Manure Management Programme, its objectives are to provide fuel for cooking and improve sanitation in villages. By 2008, 96 projects were initiated that would generate about 650 megawatts of power. The biomass materials used in these projects include rice, husk, cotton stalk, cane trash, and poultry litter.

Energy from the Lap of Nature

Achievements so far

- Between 1961 and 1973, that is, within a span of twelve years, 7,000 biogas plants were installed in India.
- So far, more than four million biogas plants have been installed in the country.
- The Indian Institute of Technology, Delhi, has carried out research on different types of biomass materials. People working on this project collected around 450 samples of different biomass materials and published a reference book for researchers and developers in the field.
- Madurai Kamaraj University, Madurai, has developed and adapted biomass gasifiers to high-temperature appliances used in the ceramic and aluminium industries.
- In 1994, the HCL Agro Biomass Power Plant became the first biomass power project to be sanctioned by the government. The equipment for the plant was imported from China.
- The Indo-Lahri Biomass Power Project was the second biomass power project to be sanctioned by the Government of India. Indigenous equipment was used in this project.
- The Indian Institute of Science (IISc), Bangalore, has developed a system for cleaning biogas plants. The centre has also transferred the technology to a number of commercial manufacturers.

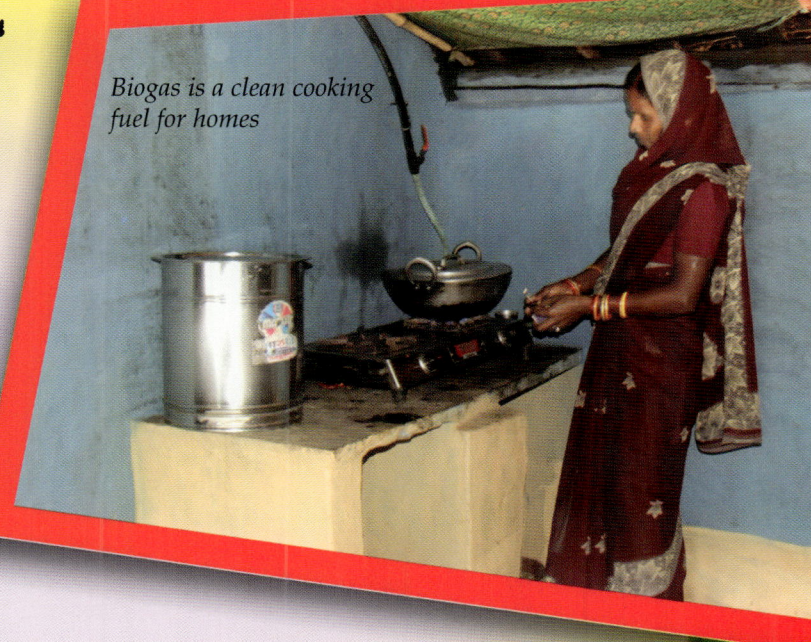
Biogas is a clean cooking fuel for homes

A biogas producing unit using waste to produce fuel

Glossary

algae: simple, primitive plants found in water or on damp surfaces. They can photosynthesize their own food.

bagasse: the waste left behind after juice is removed from sugar cane. It is used to make bioethanol.

bio-diesel: biofuel that is blended with diesel and used in diesel engine vehicles.

biofuel: fuel produced from organic matter.

fuel: anything that has energy and can be converted to another form of energy. For example, coal and petroleum are fuels.

jatropha: an evergreen shrub with seeds that hold a high amount of oil that can be converted into bio-diesel.

methanol: the simplest form of alcohol, often made from natural gas.

palm oil: oil from the fruit of the oil palm tree, used to make bio-diesel.

pyrolysis: one way to convert biomass into bio-diesel using heat.

syngas: short for synthetic gas, it is a mixture of carbon monoxide and hydrogen.

switchgrass: a hardy grass found in North America. It is used to make ethanol.

tallow: animal fat; it can be made into bio-diesel.

yeast: single-celled fungus that ferments carbohydrates. Fermenting sugar with yeast gives bioethanol.

Index

bagasse 10

biofuel
    biofuel crops 25
    bio-diesel 13, 18, 19, 20, 24, 25, 26, 27

diesel 18, 19

dung 6, 7, 11, 12, 13, 15, 25

ethanol 9, 10, 11, 17, 18, 20, 21, 23

Ford 20

genetically engineered crops 25

jatropha 18, 19

landfill gas 22, 23

methane 8, 12, 17, 22, 23

methanol 17, 20, 22

pyrolysis 21

short rotation coppice 16

syngas 21

Veggie van 27